GRAPHIC LIBRARY™

ROCKS

AND THE PEOPLE WHO LOVE THEM

BY NEL YOMTOV

ILLUSTRATED BY TIMOTHY FOSS

CAPSTONE PRESS
a capstone imprint

Graphic Library is published by Capstone Press,
1710 Roe Crest Drive, North Mankato, Minnesota 56003.
www.capstonepub.com

Books published by Capstone Press are manufactured with paper
containing at least 10 percent post-consumer waste.

Library of Congress Cataloging-in-Publication Data
Yomtov, Nelson.
  Rocks and the people who love them / by Nel Yomtov ; illustrated by Timothy Foss.
    p. cm.—(Graphic library. adventures in science)
  Includes bibliographical references and index.
  Summary: "In graphic novel format, explores igneous, sedimentary, and metamorphic rock,
discusses the rock cycle and uses of rock, and highlights the scientists who study rocks"—
Provided by publisher.
  ISBN 978-1-4296-7687-8 (library binding)
  ISBN 978-1-4296-7988-6 (paperback)
  1. Rock—Juvenile literature. 2. Rocks—Identification—Juvenile literature. 3. Petrology—
Juvenile literature. I. Foss, Timothy. II. Title. III. Series.
  QE432.2Y66 2012
  552—dc23   2011028735

Art Director
Nathan Gassman

Designer
Lori Bye

Editor
Christopher L. Harbo

Production Specialist
Laura Manthe

Consultant:
Bryce Hoppie, PhD
Professor of Geology
Minnesota State University, Mankato

The author wishes to dedicate this book to the memory of Willy DeVille.

Printed in the United States of America in Stevens Point, Wisconsin.
102011   006404WZS12

TABLE OF CONTENTS

Earth formed about 4.5 billion years ago.

It wasn't until about 200 years ago that scientists began understanding the forces that shaped our planet.

For centuries, its origin remained a mystery to people.

With that knowledge, they uncovered the origin and makeup of Earth's most common feature.

Rock—the solid material beneath our feet . . .

... the massive walls of a mountain cliff ...

... the millions of pebbles on an ocean beach ...

... and the countless natural wonders that dot our planet's surface.

But what exactly are rocks? And how do rocks become rocks in the first place?

Rocks are all around us, but we don't often think about what they're made of.

Most rocks are made up of combinations of minerals. Minerals are solids made of chemical elements, such as carbon, iron, and aluminum.

Earth has thousands of minerals, but only a few minerals make up most rocks.

The most common rock-forming minerals are quartz, olivine, feldspar, hornblende, augite, and mica.

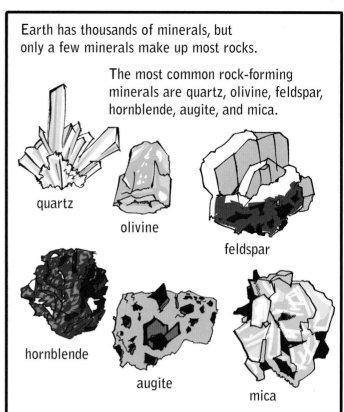

quartz

olivine

feldspar

hornblende

augite

mica

To understand how rock becomes rock, we have to dig a little deeper. Deeper into Earth, that is. Our planet is made up of four layers.

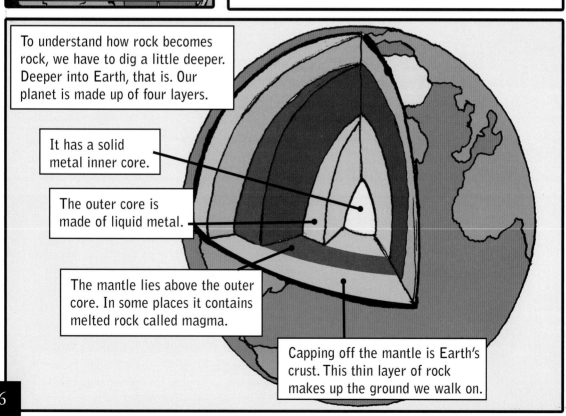

It has a solid metal inner core.

The outer core is made of liquid metal.

The mantle lies above the outer core. In some places it contains melted rock called magma.

Capping off the mantle is Earth's crust. This thin layer of rock makes up the ground we walk on.

When it comes to forming rocks, Earth's mantle and crust make it happen.

Rocks form by pressure, heat, ...

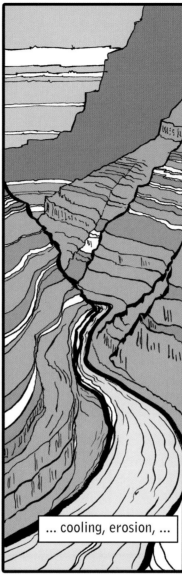

... cooling, erosion, ...

... and weathering within Earth and on its surface.

But not all rocks are created equal. Scientists group rock into three classes—igneous, sedimentary, and metamorphic.

CHAPTER 2 RED-HOT ROCKS

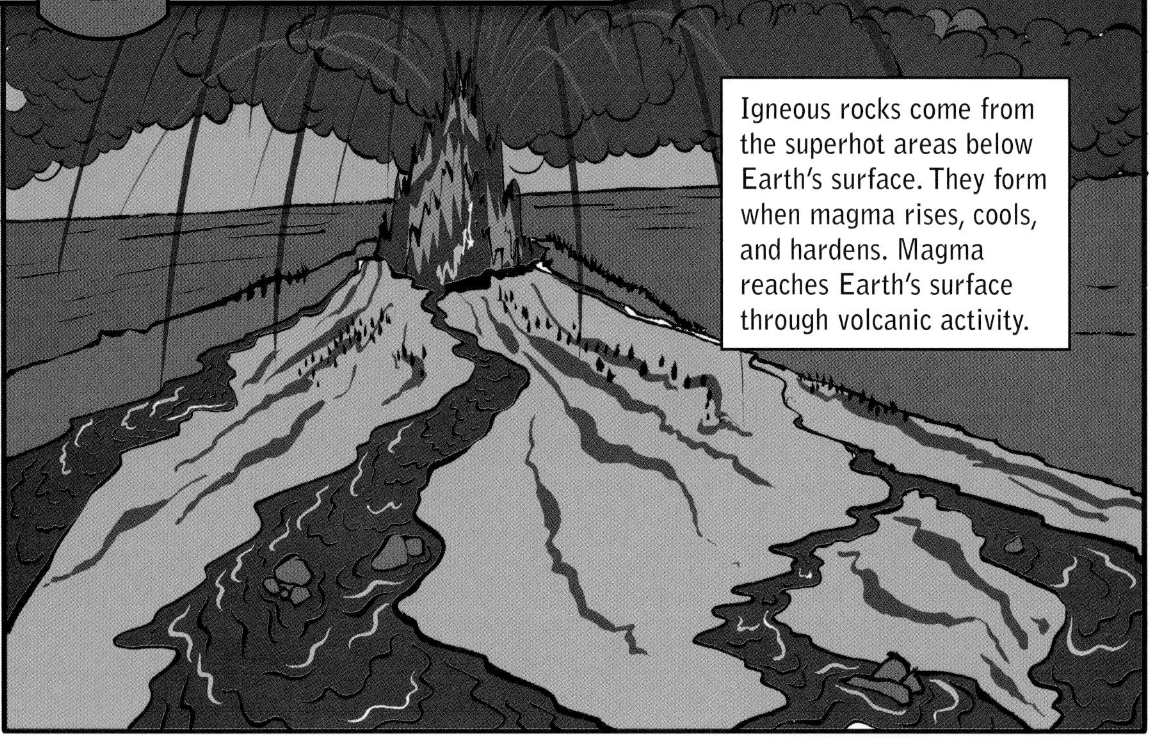
Igneous rocks come from the superhot areas below Earth's surface. They form when magma rises, cools, and hardens. Magma reaches Earth's surface through volcanic activity.

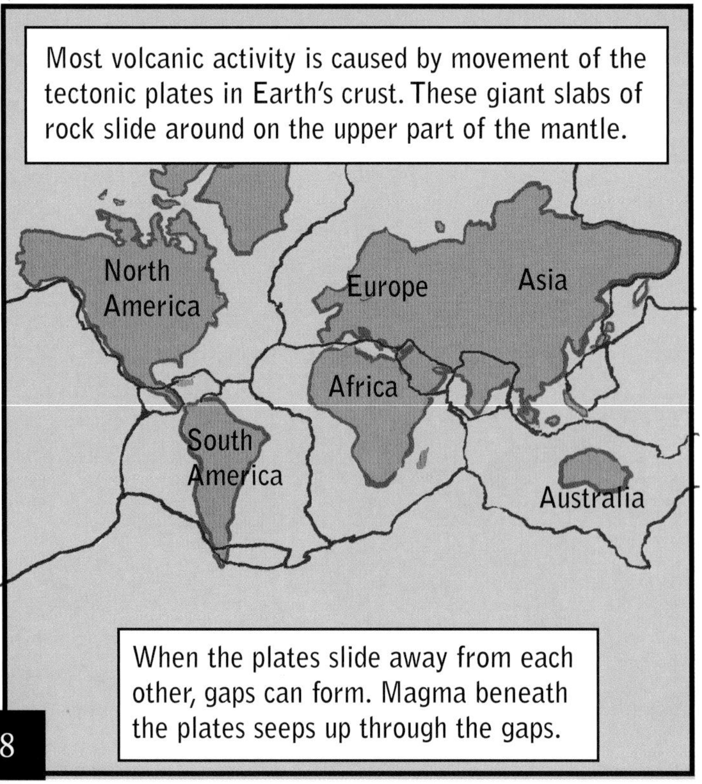
Most volcanic activity is caused by movement of the tectonic plates in Earth's crust. These giant slabs of rock slide around on the upper part of the mantle.
North America
Europe
Asia
Africa
South America
Australia
When the plates slide away from each other, gaps can form. Magma beneath the plates seeps up through the gaps.

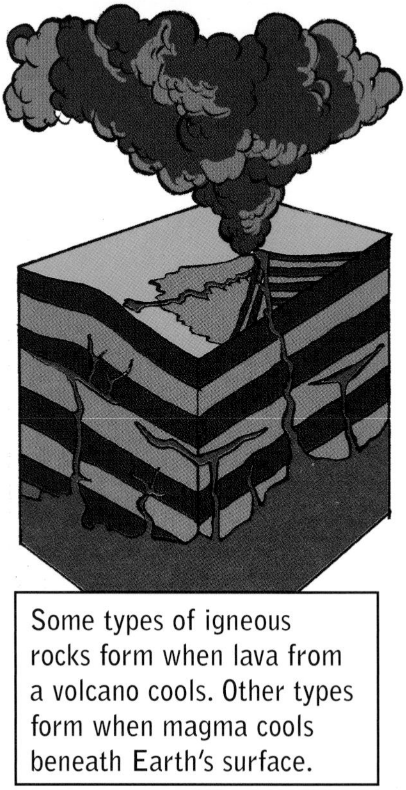
Some types of igneous rocks form when lava from a volcano cools. Other types form when magma cools beneath Earth's surface.

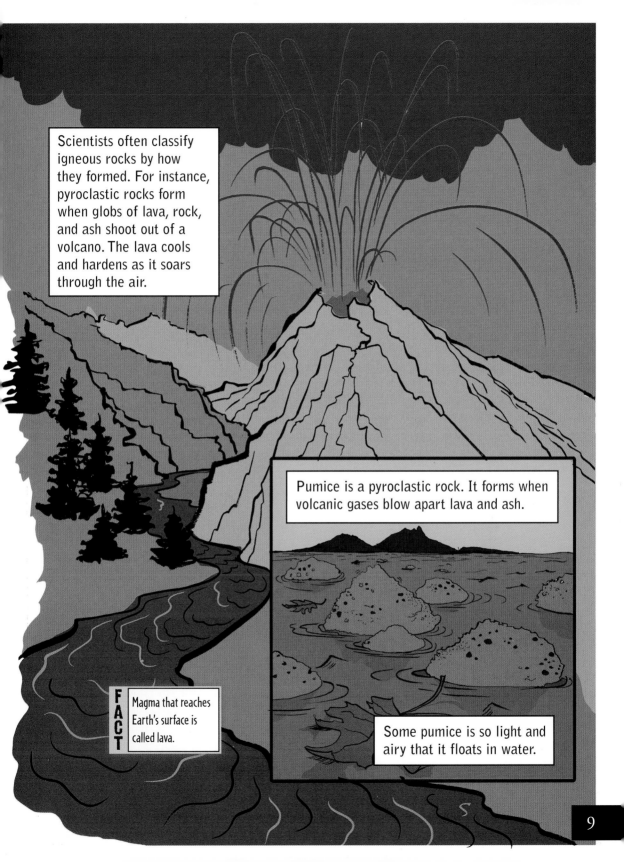

Scientists often classify igneous rocks by how they formed. For instance, pyroclastic rocks form when globs of lava, rock, and ash shoot out of a volcano. The lava cools and hardens as it soars through the air.

Pumice is a pyroclastic rock. It forms when volcanic gases blow apart lava and ash.

FACT Magma that reaches Earth's surface is called lava.

Some pumice is so light and airy that it floats in water.

Some igneous rocks form when lava creeps down a volcano during an eruption. Felsic lava is thick and sticky. It flows slowly and cools into sheets of sharp-edged rocks.

Some types of felsic lava form pale-colored rhyolite.

Other kinds form darker, glassy-looking obsidian.

Mafic lava often behaves differently. It can flow quickly and spread over large areas.

Some rocks formed by mafic lava have a smooth surface. They look like rope.

Basalt forms from mafic lava. It is one of the most common rocks on Earth.

Giant's Causeway in Ireland is one of the most remarkable rock formations in the world. It is made up of about 40,000 columns of basalt rock.

The columns formed when lava cooled and hardened very rapidly.

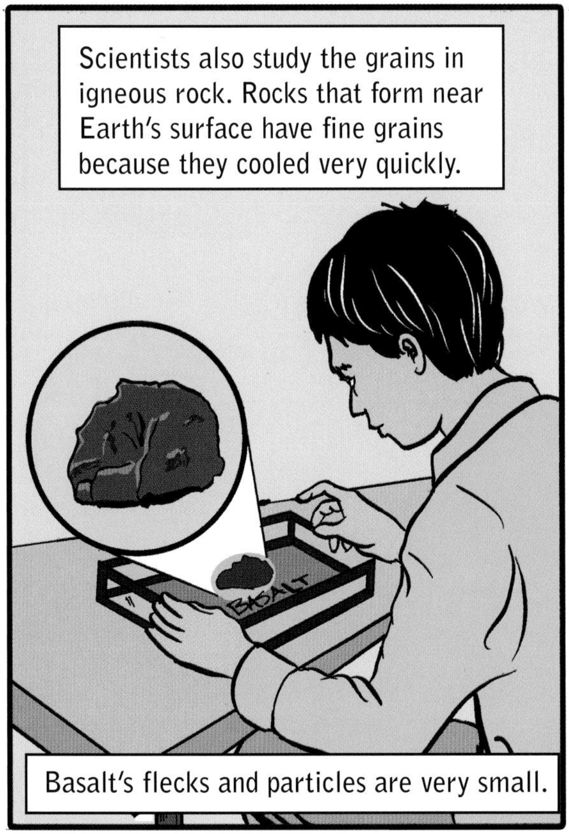
Scientists also study the grains in igneous rock. Rocks that form near Earth's surface have fine grains because they cooled very quickly.
BASALT
Basalt's flecks and particles are very small.

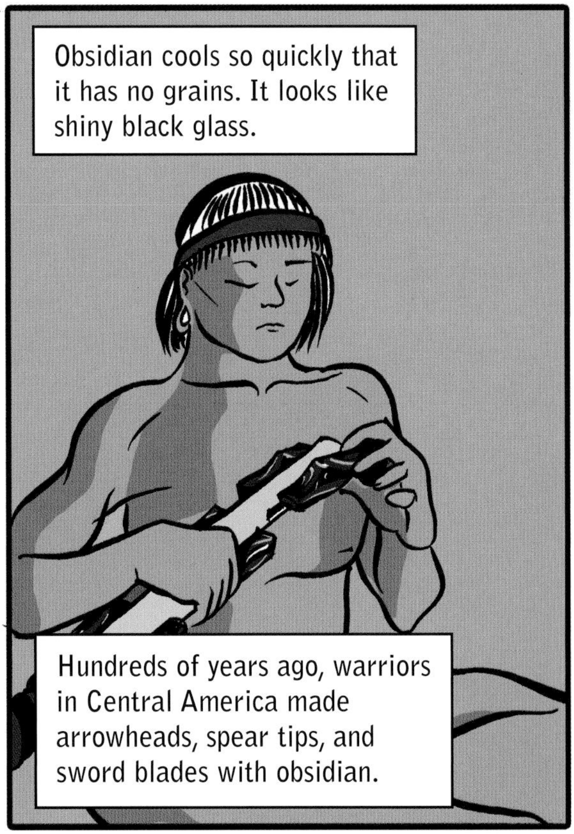
Obsidian cools so quickly that it has no grains. It looks like shiny black glass.
Hundreds of years ago, warriors in Central America made arrowheads, spear tips, and sword blades with obsidian.

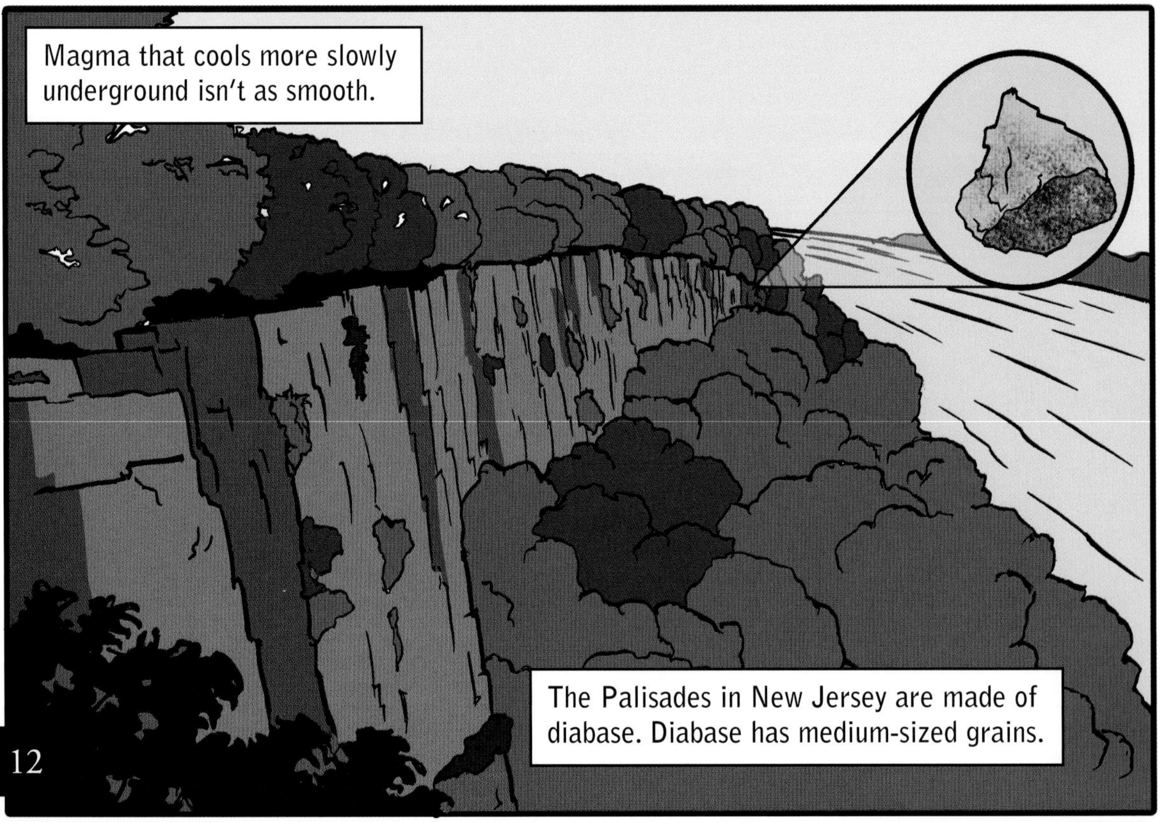
Magma that cools more slowly underground isn't as smooth.
The Palisades in New Jersey are made of diabase. Diabase has medium-sized grains.

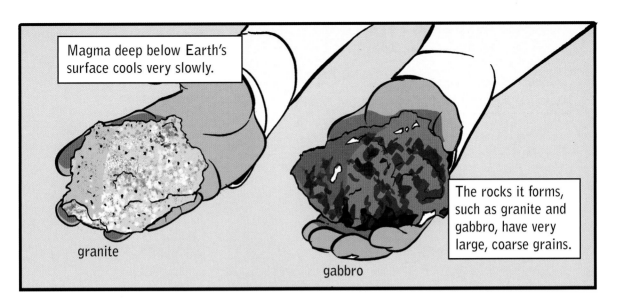

Magma deep below Earth's surface cools very slowly.

The rocks it forms, such as granite and gabbro, have very large, coarse grains.

granite

gabbro

GEOLOGISTS AT WORK

Geologists love rocks so much they have special fields of study. A geomorphologist investigates how wind, water, and ice shape rocks and land. Volcanologists check out volcano eruptions, lava, and magma. An environmental geologist uses the study of rocks to fight pollution and protect water and land.

CHAPTER 3

PILING UP THE LAYERS

While igneous rocks have red-hot origins, sedimentary rock forms in gentler ways. As you can tell by its name, sedimentary rock is made of sediment.

Sediment is weathered and broken-down pieces of rocks, minerals, plants, and animals.

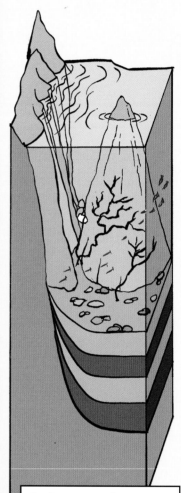

Sediment settles in swamps, lakes, oceans, or riverbeds. It builds up in layers over thousands or millions of years. Eventually, the sediment becomes cemented together and forms rock.

FACT
Sedimentary rock makes up about 75 percent of the rocks seen on land.

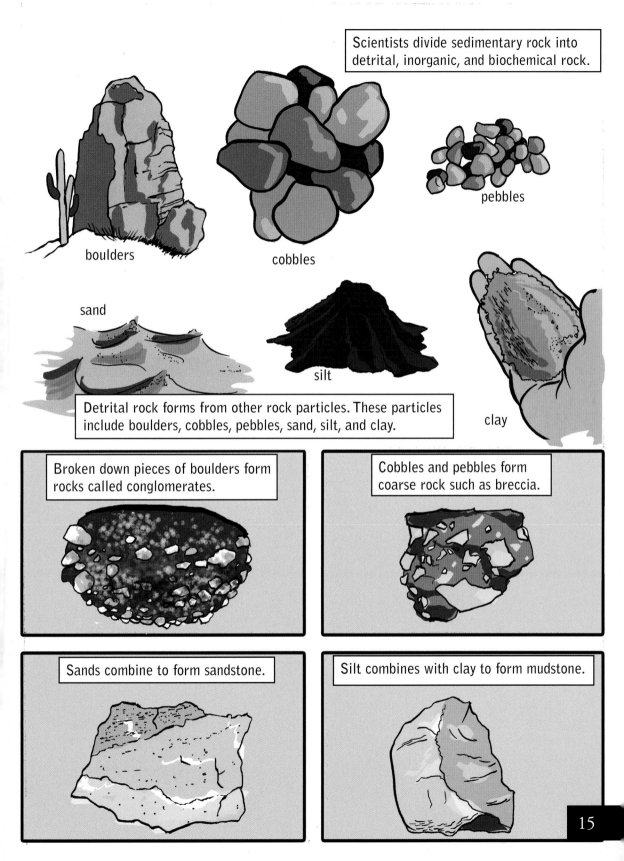

Scientists divide sedimentary rock into detrital, inorganic, and biochemical rock.

boulders

cobbles

pebbles

sand

silt

clay

Detrital rock forms from other rock particles. These particles include boulders, cobbles, pebbles, sand, silt, and clay.

Broken down pieces of boulders form rocks called conglomerates.

Cobbles and pebbles form coarse rock such as breccia.

Sands combine to form sandstone.

Silt combines with clay to form mudstone.

15

Inorganic rocks form from minerals that dissolve in water.

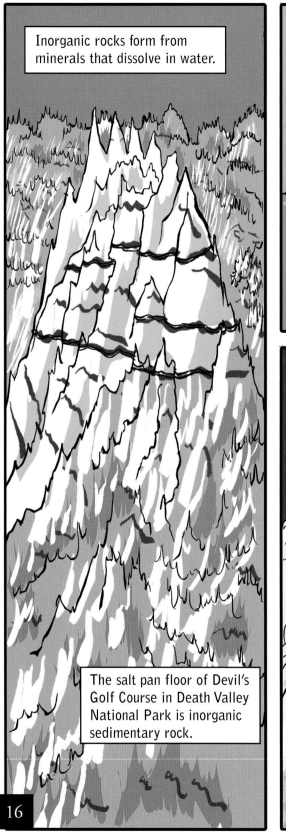

The salt pan floor of Devil's Golf Course in Death Valley National Park is inorganic sedimentary rock.

Mono Lake, California, is home to calcite rocks called tufa towers.

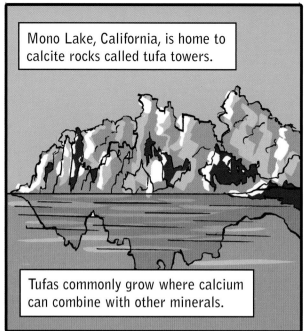

Tufas commonly grow where calcium can combine with other minerals.

At Pamukkale Falls in Turkey, minerals in the water form a soft jelly. The jelly hardens into travertine, a beautiful building stone.

FACT Pamukkale means "cotton castle" in Turkish.

The stalactites and stalagmites in caves are made from the mineral calcite. They form when rainwater seeps into the ground and dissolves limestone.

SPACE ROCKS

Earth isn't the only place in the universe that has rocks. Billions of rocks swirl around in space. Most rocks burn up when they enter Earth's atmosphere. But meteorites are rocks that crash-land and create craters on Earth. Meteorites are made of stone and iron.

Biochemical sedimentary rocks are graveyards of the dead. They form when plant and animal remains pile up and harden.

England's White Cliffs of Dover formed when the remains of tiny plants and animals stacked up on the ocean floor. Over millions of years, they hardened into chalk.

Coral reefs are limestones made from the skeletons of sea creatures.

Because sedimentary rocks pile up in layers, they often hold fossils.

Fossilized plant leaves show us the remains of an ancient forest.

Fossils are the remains of animals or plants preserved as rock.

Dinosaur fossils show how the animal's soft parts rotted away. The bones hardened into rock.

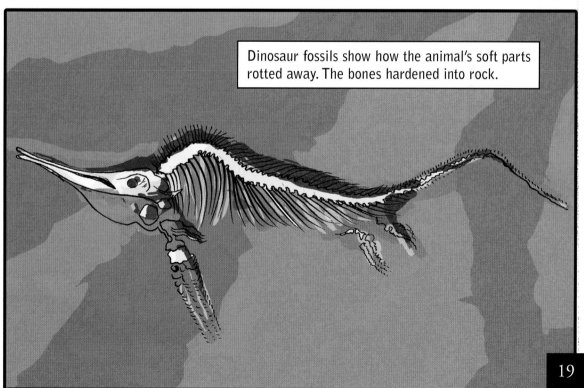

CHAPTER 4

THE PRESSURE IS ON

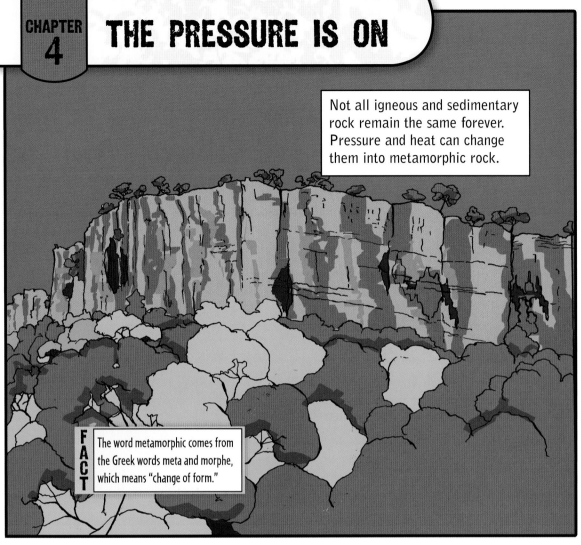

Not all igneous and sedimentary rock remain the same forever. Pressure and heat can change them into metamorphic rock.

FACT The word metamorphic comes from the Greek words meta and morphe, which means "change of form."

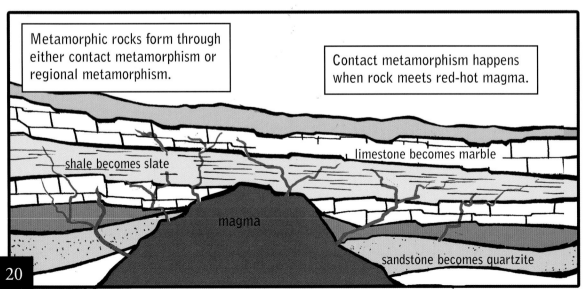

Metamorphic rocks form through either contact metamorphism or regional metamorphism.

Contact metamorphism happens when rock meets red-hot magma.

shale becomes slate

limestone becomes marble

magma

sandstone becomes quartzite

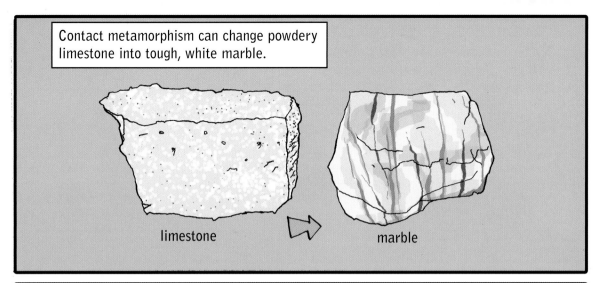

Contact metamorphism can change powdery limestone into tough, white marble.

limestone → marble

Sandstone is a sedimentary rock made of quartz sand.

sandstone → quartzite

With extreme heat and pressure, sandstone becomes durable quartzite.

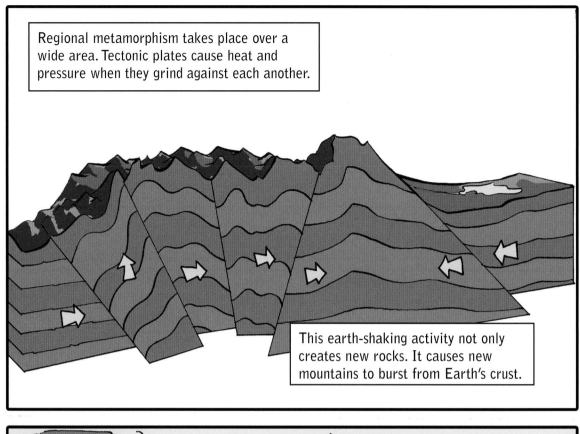

Regional metamorphism takes place over a wide area. Tectonic plates cause heat and pressure when they grind against each another.

This earth-shaking activity not only creates new rocks. It causes new mountains to burst from Earth's crust.

The incredible pressure and heat of regional metamorphism create rocks with dynamic characteristics. Foliated rocks have flat or wavy dark lines.

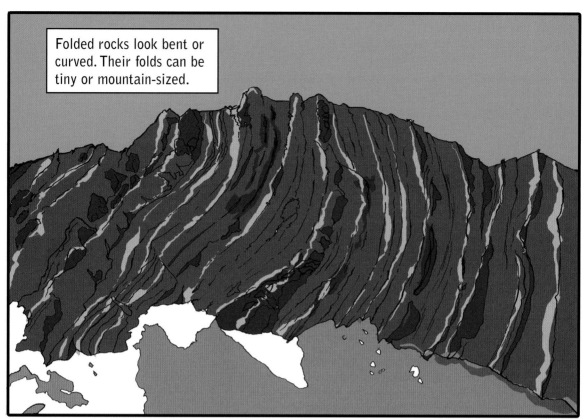

Folded rocks look bent or curved. Their folds can be tiny or mountain-sized.

The pressure of regional metamorphosis can even change the arrangement of a rock's minerals. This change results in splits in rocks.

The brute power of regional metamorphism creates some of the most stunning rock features on Earth.

South America's Andes Mountains formed when heat and pressure changed sedimentary rock into quartzite and slate.

Metamorphism changed limestone into the marble in Carrara, Italy.

Sea shells in the limestone give Carrara marble its brilliant white color.

Carrara marble was prized by famous sculptors for its purity and beauty.

SO YOU WANT TO BE A GEOLOGIST?

If rocks rock your world, you might want to become a geologist. All it takes is an interest in the environment and attention to detail. Many types of industries use geologists, including oil, gas, and mining. These geologists use their knowledge of rocks to discover new fuel deposits. Some geologists work in research or teach at universities.

Between 1501 and 1504, Michelangelo sculpted his famous statue *David* from a single block of white Carrara marble.

CHAPTER 5

THE ENDLESS SUPPLY OF ROCKS

Even if you don't always notice it, rocks slowly and steadily change.

The forces of nature wear away all rock. Erosion breaks down rocks with the relentless force of waves, running water, and ice.

Even gentle rainfalls, air, and very hot and cold temperatures can break down rock.

When a rock breaks down without being moved, the process is called weathering.

Chemical weathering occurs when rainwater mixes with chemicals in the air. The water dissolves minerals in a rock.

The rock wears down or its color or texture changes.

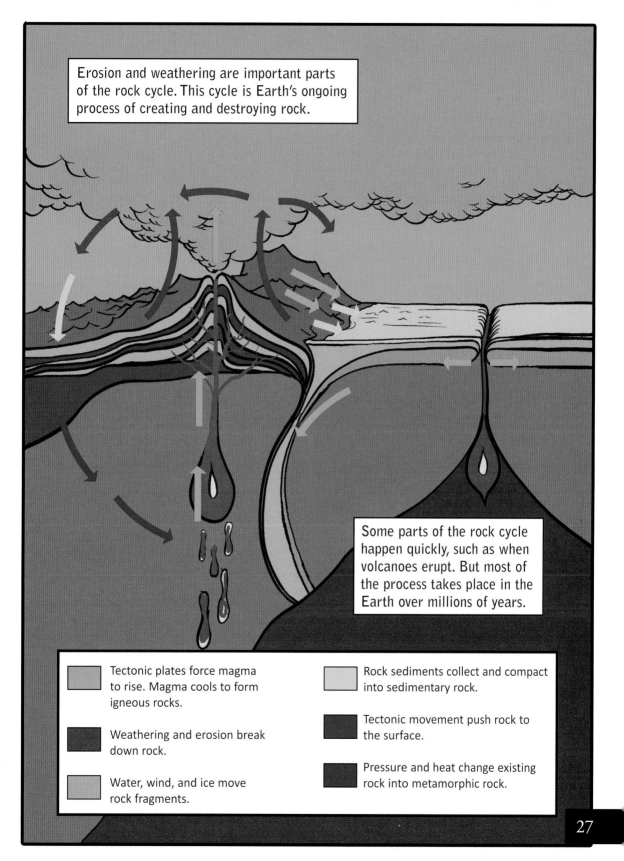

Erosion and weathering are important parts of the rock cycle. This cycle is Earth's ongoing process of creating and destroying rock.

Some parts of the rock cycle happen quickly, such as when volcanoes erupt. But most of the process takes place in the Earth over millions of years.

Tectonic plates force magma to rise. Magma cools to form igneous rocks.

Weathering and erosion break down rock.

Water, wind, and ice move rock fragments.

Rock sediments collect and compact into sedimentary rock.

Tectonic movement push rock to the surface.

Pressure and heat change existing rock into metamorphic rock.

Throughout history, people have used rocks as weapons, work tools, building stones, and decorations.

Igneous rocks such as diorite and rhyolite were often made into battle-axes or digging tools.

Chunks of hard, sedimentary flint splits. Its sharp edges made ideal weapons or cutting tools.

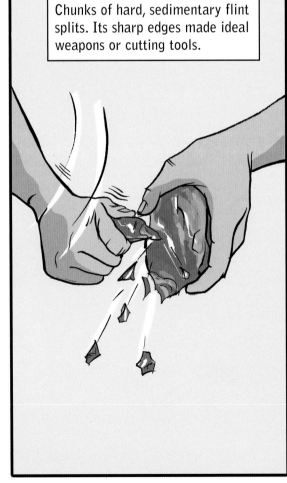

The heads of four U.S. presidents were carved into the smooth granite of Mount Rushmore in South Dakota.

FACT The granite at Mount Rushmore erodes only 1 inch (2.5 centimeters) every 10,000 years.

Sedimentary rock such as sandstone and limestone are easy to dig up and carve.

The Great Pyramid of Egypt and the Great Sphinx were built with limestone.

Rocks play an important role in our everyday lives.

They are useful. They add beauty to the world. And best of all, they tell an amazing story about the history and science of our planet.

29

GLOSSARY

erosion (i-ROH-zhuhn)—the wearing away of land by water or wind

foliated (FOH-lee-ey-tid)—rock that has wavy bands of color

fossil (FAH-suhl)—the remains or traces of plants and animals that are preserved as rock

igneous rock (IG-nee-uhss ROK)—rocks formed when magma cools and hardens

lava (LAH-vuh)—the hot, liquid rock that pours out of a volcano when it erupts

magma (MAG-muh)—melted rock found under the earth's surface

metamorphic rock (met-uh-MOR-fik ROK)—rock that is changed by heat and pressure

metamorphism (met-uh-MOR-fiz-uhm)—the process of changing appearance or form

sedimentary rock (sed-uh-MEN-tuh-ree ROK)—rock formed by layers of rocks, sand, or clay that have been pressed together

tectonic plates (tek-TON-ik PLAYTES)—gigantic slabs of Earth's crust that move around on magma

weathering (WETH-ur-ing)—breaking down of solid rock into smaller and smaller pieces by wind, water, glaciers, or plant roots

READ MORE

Hoffman, Steven M. *Rock Study: A Guide to Looking at Rocks*. Rock It! New York: PowerKids Press, 2011.

Korb, Rena B. *Radical Rocks*. Science Rocks! Edina, Minn.: Magic Wagon, 2008.

Rice, William B. *Rocks and Minerals*. Mission, Science. Mankato, Minn.: Compass Point Books, 2009.

Walker, Kate. *Rocks*. Investigating Earth. New York: Marshall Cavendish Benchmark, 2012.

INTERNET SITES

FactHound offers a safe, fun way to find Internet sites related to this book. All of the sites on FactHound have been researched by our staff.

Here's all you do:

Visit www.facthound.com

Type in this code: 9781429676878

INDEX